Dear Shruti,
Live your blissful calling!
Aymee

© Dr. Aymee Coget 2020

Cover design by Moenja Schijven

FIND YOUR BLISSFUL CALLING

by Dr. Aymee Coget

Sustainable Happiness Expert

The founder of the five step formula to sustainable happiness

Start your heart-based professional path today!

DEDICATION

This workbook is dedicated to my family who encouraged me to follow my heart in life. It is for everyone looking to fill an emptiness inside and longing for clarity in their professional path. This workbook is dedicated to the brave who dare to listen to the voice within.

WHAT ARE PEOPLE SAYING?

If you or someone you are mentoring/coaching/teaching/guiding is in search of their calling (the answer to that vital yet often plaguing question, "What am I meant to be doing with my life?!"), you have found the essential tool for eliciting that answer through this comprehensive workbook. Dr. Coget combines years of clinical research and expert experience in the field of positive psychology and leadership to provide a systematic, simplified approach to unearthing one's "Blissful Calling". She teaches the differences between a job, a career, and a calling, and her reflective activities help you tap into the teacher within that guides you in unlocking the awareness of your passion, strengths, and path to a meaningful, altruistic profession. I am forever grateful for Dr. Coget in helping me discover my Blissful Calling (which is now 100% realized and helping the world at large!), and it is with the biggest smile that I give the highest recommendation for this life-changing, soul-aligning resource!

- Jessica Boote, San Francisco, CA

Before my Blissful Calling exercise I was having conflict around what I was needing in my professional world. I realized the type of work I was doing was impacting my physical body and mental health in a negative way, and I had to take a look at changing what I was doing. I was scared to imagine that what I thought was a good fit for me could actually be causing me harm. What did this mean for my working life? It was hard to imagine a pathway that would help me figure out what I was needing moving forward. Then, through the support of Aymee I found the Blissful Calling exercise.

As I started the Blissful Calling exercise I found the separation of job, career, and calling to be very helpful. I knew that I had a calling to work with others directly to promote healing, growth and wellbeing. This understanding of my path as a calling helped me to find some flexibility in the way I looked at my work. There are many different things I could be doing that still aligned with my calling and allowed me to leave the job that was negatively impacting me. One of my favorite parts of this exercise was the guided visualization of what I would be experiencing in this calling, and it helped me to create an image of what I was wanting and looking for. It's funny to me now, that during the process I felt overwhelmed by the knowledge that I would have to describe my blissful calling in two words. Of course, in a magical way, when I got to that part of the exercise the answer came to me without question and has led me to where I am now.

It has been a little over a year since I embarked on the Blissful Calling exercise, and a few months ago I caught myself between sessions in a moment that I had only imagined in my visualization. I was working a full day filled with clients I enjoy, sipping delicious tea in my office that I have adorned with plants and things that make me happy. I realized that I had fully stepped into my blissful calling, and what seemed like would once take forever was now already here. The process has felt magical and also chosen. I am extremely grateful for this support on my journey!

- Madeline Sharp, LCSW-C, Gaithersburg, MD

Dr. Aymee Coget's Blissful Calling workbook is an excellent tool for determining your true calling. What is special about this guide is that it is scientifically backed by what actually makes people happy. It integrates character strengths, passion and your hearts deepest desires, it asks a full spectrum of questions that enable you to hone in on what you really want out of a profession ranging from how much responsibility you would like, to what types of skills you would like to utilize. I would highly recommend this workbook for anyone who is ready to take action with prioritizing their perfect profession.

- Emily Oliver, Sarasota, FL

TABLE OF CONTENTS

INTRODUCTION: FINDING YOUR HEART'S BLISSFUL CALLING 4
    HEART'S VOICE VS. MIND'S VOICE EXERCISE 5

CHAPTER ONE: PUT ON YOUR GANDHI HAT 8
    HEART EXERCISE 9

CHAPTER TWO: CREATE YOUR PASSION INDEX 11
    PASSION EXERCISE 12

CHAPTER THREE: WHAT COMES NATURALLY TO ME? 15
    VIA STRENGTHS 15
    STRENGTHS & SKILLS EXERCISE 16

CHAPTER FOUR: JOB, CAREER OR CALLING 17
    ILLUMINATE YOUR TRUTH EXERCISE 18

CHAPTER FIVE: YOUR BLISSFUL CALLING VISION 20
    YOUR BLISSFUL CALLING MOVIE EXERCISE 21
    YOUR BLISSFUL CALLING ACTION PLAN 25

REFERENCES 31

ABOUT THE AUTHOR 36

INTRODUCTION: FINDING YOUR HEART'S BLISSFUL CALLING

We can use all the happiness skills possible to create our happy home lives and happy social lives, yet we can still find ourselves facing dissatisfaction within one other major part of our life: our WORK! If we hate our jobs, what is the point in doing all of this work in creating a happy life?

Perhaps you went to college, chose to forego it, or were without the opportunity to attend. Regardless of the circumstances, you probably found yourself stumbling around and haphazardly deciding on your profession.

The process of finding your blissful calling is one that will knock your socks off! Instead of continuing to allow your experiences, education, parents, and other outside circumstances to dictate your professional decisions, these following exercises will show you how to make CHOICES FROM YOUR HEART.

HEART'S VOICE VS. MIND'S VOICE EXERCISE

Take a few moments to ask yourself, "What did I do today?"

Write down the answer.

_____
_____
_____
_____

Likely, this answer is a bullet pointed to-do list. Now let's consider accessing the voice in your heart to answer this same question. The heart's voice is different than your general 'go to' which is your tendency- the voice in your mind. This exercise will teach you how to go inside your heart to hear its truth.

This is going to be a self-meditative state so make sure you are in a room by yourself and will be undisturbed. Record the following instructions and play it back to yourself when you're ready.

_____

"Put both feet on the ground.
Close your eyes.
Place one hand on your heart and one hand on your belly.
Take a deep breath,
One more time for good measure.
Drop your awareness into your heart center.
Focus your attention in the area of your heart.
Focus on creating an
all loving, all nurturing, all accepting,
open environment.
Then allow your heartbeat to come through your chest to the palm of your hand.

When you can feel your heartbeat, ask yourself, to your heart,
'What did I do today?'
Wait for the response.
When the response comes, ask,
'Anything else?'
Continue to ask for anything else until your heart is complete.
When you are ready, you can bring your awareness back to here and now."

Write down the answers from your heart's inquiry.

Do you notice a difference?

There are often different answers between your heart and your mind to the same question. Are you ready to approach your professional life from the consideration of your heart? This is the natural voice within that is your access to the deepest wisdom of your soul. As you tune into your heart's voice, let us introduce the definitions of **"Blissful"** and **"Calling"**:

Blissful \ 'blis-fəl \ "full of, marked by, or causing complete happiness"[1]

Calling \ 'ko-liŋ \ "a strong inner impulse toward a particular course of action especially when accompanied by conviction of [the greater good]"[2]

In sustainable happiness, bliss is the highest level of happiness before a state of lower nirvana. We aim to achieve this state from feeling connected to a spiritual source larger than us i.e. the ocean, nature, yoga, meditation, church, prayer, a music concert, etc. When we feel this connected sense of oneness with 'all that is', we achieve a state of bliss.

[1] "Blissful", 2020

[2] "Calling", 2020

What if you could actually be blissful at work?

That is our plan!

A calling is an authentic, professional role where you feel in service and connected to the bigger picture of life. We designed the following step-by-step format so you can find your blissful calling.

The key is to ask and answer the questions throughout the workbook from your HEART.

CHAPTER ONE:
PUT ON YOUR GHANDI HAT

Mahatma Gandhi (1869 – 1948) is one of the greatest political and spiritual leaders of our past. He is lovingly known in India as the "Father of the Nation" in honor of his work in liberating the country from the British Empire after a 30-year campaign. His leadership stands out in history due to his benevolent method of fighting without violence or retaliation which he called "Satyagraha". This philosophy remarkably resulted in allies on both sides after India won their independence and continues to inspire international freedom and civil rights movements.

HEART EXERCISE

One of Gandhi's more famous quotes is, "Be the change you want to see in the world."

In this exercise, you will tap into your heart's voice to discover the change you want to see in the world (beyond what your head maybe telling you).

Record the following instructions and play it back to yourself in a place where you are alone and will be undisturbed.

"Take a deep breath, eyes are closed.

Put one hand on your heart, one hand on your belly.

Take another deep breath.

Drop your attention into your heart center.

Focus your awareness into the area of your heart.

Focus on creating an all loving, all nurturing and all accepting,

open environment there.

Allow your heartbeat to come through your chest to the palm of your hand. When you

feel your heartbeat ask to yourself, to your heart,

'What is the change I want to see in the world?'

Wait for a response to come from your heart.

When the answer comes to you, ask, 'Anything else?'

Wait for a response.

Repeat, 'Anything else?'

Wait for the response.

Continue to ask, 'Anything else?' until your heart is complete."

List below the changes your heart would like to see in the world.

_____
_____
_____
_____
_____
_____

Take time to reflect on your heart's answers. Embrace it. Become it.

CHAPTER TWO: CREATE YOUR PASSION INDEX

How many passionate people do you know?

Most people would say very few. What does the word "passion" mean anyway?

Passion is any powerful or compelling emotion or feeling.

One way to skip small talk with new acquaintances at social gatherings is to ask them what they are passionate about. It is interesting to see the responses. Sometimes the answer is dull and boring because the person is out of touch with their passions. However, now they are thinking about it... If the person does have people, places, things, activities, or causes they are passionate about, their energy totally shifts into the excitement of sharing their passion.

PASSION EXERCISE

To gauge what you are passionate about, start logging when you experience an intense emotion.

Who was there?

_____
_____
_____
_____
_____
_____

What were you talking about?

_____
_____
_____
_____
_____
_____

Why did you respond so intensely?

_____
_____
_____
_____
_____
_____

Reflect on the last time you felt an extreme emotion and describe the situation below.

_____
_____
_____
_____
_____
_____

Who was there?

_____
_____
_____
_____
_____
_____

What were you talking about?

_____
_____
_____
_____
_____
_____

Why did you respond so intensely?

_____
_____
_____
_____
_____
_____

Why did you feel so emotionally connected to the situation?

_____
_____
_____
_____
_____
_____

Considering the answers to your questions above, what are you passionate about?

_____
_____
_____
_____
_____
_____

Right now you can repeat the process for reflecting on other times you remember experiencing extreme emotions. Or going forward, you can start a passion journal and begin logging the situations you experience (positive or negative) to identify the things, people, and topics that ignite intense emotions in you. This reflection will increase your awareness of what topics you are passionate about.

CHAPTER THREE:
WHAT COMES NATURALLY TO ME?

VIA STRENGTHS

Go to www.viacharacter.org/survey/account/register, where you can take the VIA Character Strengths Survey in order to identify your top strengths. After completing the survey, write down your top five strengths.

1. _____
2. _____
3. _____
4. _____
5. _____

Research shows, when we have strengths as part of our self-concept, we are happier.

Let's think about how you can use your strengths in a work context.

STRENGTHS & SKILLS EXERCISE

We have addressed what you care about and identified your passionate topics.

Your strengths determine what skills comes naturally.

Make a chart on a piece of paper and BRAINSTORM:

Top 5 Strengths	Behaviors related to strengths	Skills related to behaviors	Activities related to behaviors & skills

CHAPTER FOUR:
JOB, CAREER OR CALLING

Many people wake up when the alarm goes off, moan and groan, and loathe getting out of bed because they detest their jobs. The only reason they go to work in the first place is because they have to pay the bills.

Others wake up when the alarm goes off and immediately think they have to hurry, get in the shower, put on a suit, and run to work so they can get promoted quickly. They kind of like their job. They potentially studied the topic matter in college. They feel secure yet they are very motivated to move up the ladder.

Lastly there is a group of people who view their profession as a calling. A calling feels like you are doing work for the greater good of humanity, and there is a sense of spiritual purpose in accomplishing it. The people who feel like they have a calling are more satisfied with their professions and experience a high level of happiness and contentment.

Which is your path?

Job? Career? or Calling?

ILLUMINATE YOUR TRUTH EXERCISE

Do you want a job?

A job focuses on the material benefits of work instead of meaning and fulfillment. The work is simply a means to a financial end that allows people to enjoy their time away from work. The interests and ambitions of those with jobs are expressed outside of work and involve hobbies and other interests.

Make a list below of the jobs which utilize your strengths, ignite your passion, and help create the change you want to see in the world.

_____
_____
_____
_____
_____
_____

Do you want a career?

A person who wants a career works for the rewards that accompany advancement through an organizational or occupational structure. The increased pay, prestige, and status that come with promotion and advancement are a dominant focus in their work. Advancement brings high self-esteem, increased power, and higher social standing.

Make a list below of the careers which utilize your strengths, ignite your passion, and help create the change you want to see in the world.

_____
_____
_____
_____
_____
_____

Do you have a calling?

A person with a calling "…work[s] not for financial rewards or for advancement… [Instead, they work] for the fulfillment that doing the work brings. In Callings, the work is an end in itself, and is usually associated with the belief that the work contributes to the greater good and makes the world a better place." (Wrześniewski, A. 2003. p. 301)

Make a list below of the callings which utilize your strengths, ignite your passion, and help create the change you want to see in the world.

_____
_____
_____
_____
_____
_____

Which one would you like to work toward?

_____
_____
_____
_____
_____
_____

What are the first three steps to moving toward your decision?

_____
_____
_____
_____
_____
_____

CHAPTER FIVE: YOUR BLISSFUL CALLING VISION

Acknowledge your self-awareness.

Deep down inside you are the only one who knows what really makes you feel happy.

Honor your truth without judgment and free yourself to express your inner voice.

You know yourself better than anyone else.

We are counting on this knowledge and awareness for this exercise.

Take into account the changes you want to see in the world and what you are passionate about then get ready to visualize!

Find a trusted companion and a quiet room where you can be relaxed.

Have the person read to you the following visioning exercise.

YOUR BLISSFUL CALLING MOVIE EXERCISE

To the reader: read the following passage closely and with positive intention, allowing the visualizer the time to relax and visualize.

NOTE: Leave time for each image to appear. Allow 5-10 minutes. Say each line every 20 seconds.

Speak slowly, clearly, in a relaxed, warm voice (about 1 minute)...

"Sit comfortably with your feet resting on the ground, your hands resting comfortably on your lap.

Take a deep breath and relax.

Now take another deep breath and relax even further.

You may notice there are places in your body that are stressed or tight.

Notice them... and let them go.

Continue to breathe comfortably....

As thoughts occur... notice them... and let them go.

Imagine you are walking along a seashore... The sun is shining, and you can feel the sun's warmth on your body. Continue to walk along the seashore... and relax.

Notice a door ahead of you. Open the door. There are stairs going down... Slowly descend the stairs... counting as you go...

1...... 2........3......4.......5......6......7......8......9......10.

When you reach the landing notice there is another door in front of you. On the door it says, 'Welcome to the future.' It is a very beautiful door, and you reach out with warmth and excitement to open the door and walk inside.

It is a movie theater, and you notice the movie playing is an exciting one...

It's titled 'My Blissful Calling'...

You take your seat in the theater and watch the movie.

It is a very interesting movie, showing scenes from the future of how the company you either work for or created has progressed and grown over the last several years...

You are a key player in the movie...

What cause are you working for?

What are you passionate about?

You may notice how people work together...

What types of conversations are they having?

What does the work environment look like?

Notice the people around you...

What types of things are you doing?

What gets you excited?

How do you spend your day?

Note what role you play...

What are you proud of?

What does the company feel like?

What else stands out for you?

What do others say about the company?

Who are your customers?

What are they saying?

How does it feel to hear these things?

What makes the team stand out so much?"

When you feel ready to move on… say:

"Now, it is time to end the movie and return to the present…

Keep your eyes closed, notice your breathing again…

Find yourself leaving the movie theater…

Exiting through the door and returning up the steps, counting

10…… 9…… 8…… 7…… 6

Take a deep breath and begin to feel your body awaken.

5…… 4…… 3

Notice the sounds in the room around you.

2…… 1

Open your eyes and slowly look around."

When you feel comfortable, please either write or draw as much of your vision of your future as you can. You may need to close your eyes briefly to remember parts… Make your description as whole as possible. Describe what your team (organization, etc.) will be like in the future.

_____
_____
_____
_____
_____
_____

Society de-emphasizes the importance of and search for your blissful calling.

It turns out, just as happiness must come from within, so does your blissful calling.

Write down below what you saw in your blissful calling vision.

_____
_____
_____
_____
_____
_____

YOUR BLISSFUL CALLING ACTION PLAN

This is where it all comes together!!!

Your passions, the changes you want to see, your strengths, and your vision.

What skills would you like to utilize in your job?

_____
_____
_____
_____
_____
_____

How many skills are there?

_____
_____
_____
_____
_____
_____

What types of tasks are associated with those skills?

_____
_____
_____
_____
_____
_____

How many tasks are there?

_____
_____
_____
_____
_____
_____

How significant are these tasks to your profession? Place a number 1-10 (10 is the most significant) next to the tasks to determine the significance.

_____
_____
_____
_____
_____
_____

How much autonomy do you need at work? Rate this on a scale of 1-10 with 10 being totally autonomous.

_____
_____
_____
_____
_____
_____

How much feedback do you need in order to do a good job? Rate this on a scale of 1-10 with 10 being the most possible feedback.

_____
_____
_____
_____
_____
_____

Feeling a meaningful experience is very important for a blissful calling, how would you know if you were experiencing meaningfulness at work?

_____
_____
_____
_____
_____
_____

Your work is meaningful when it gives you purpose and feels significant.

What are the intrinsic qualities of the work itself (i.e. the goals, values, and beliefs) or the organizational community within which the work is embedded?

_____
_____
_____
_____
_____
_____
_____

What are your perceptions, attitudes, and understandings of work in society, and how can they provide meaning to you?

_____
_____
_____
_____
_____
_____

Do you want responsibility at work? How much responsibility do you want to take for the outcomes of your work?

_____
_____
_____
_____
_____
_____

WHY?

_____
_____
_____
_____
_____
_____

How much feedback do you need to have at work?

_____
_____
_____
_____
_____
_____

Do you need to have knowledge about the results of your work?

_____
_____
_____
_____
_____
_____

What does this look like in the work environment?

_____
_____
_____
_____
_____
_____
_____

Given all you have considered through this portion of the course, reflect on the process you went through regarding your blissful calling.

Take a few days and mull it over then come back.

Write down how you see yourself being happy in your new blissful calling.

_____
_____
_____
_____
_____
_____

What is the name or title of your blissful calling?

_____
_____
_____

VOILA!!!!

Now you know your Blissful Calling!

REFERENCES

Abbe, A., Tkach, C., & Lyubomirsky, S. (2003). The art of living by dispositionally happy people. Journal of Happiness Studies, 4(4), 385-404.

Achor, S. (2010). The happiness advantage: How a positive brain fuels success in work and life. New York: Crown Publishing.

Ben-Shahar, T. (2007). Happier: Learn the secrets to daily joy and lasting fulfillment. New York: McGraw-Hill Education.

Berger, P. L., & Luckmann, T. (1966). The social construction of reality: A treatise in the sociology of. Knowledge. Garden City, NY: Doubleday.

Berman, J. S. (2007). Character strengths, self-schemas, and psychological well being: A multi-method approach (Doctoral dissertation).

Biswas-Diener, R. & Dean, B. (2007). Positive psychology coaching: Putting the science of happiness to work for your clients. Hoboken: John Wiley & Sons, Inc.

Biswas-Diener, R. (2010). Practicing positive psychology coaching: Assessment, activities, and strategies for success. Hoboken: John Wiley & Sons, Inc.

Blankson, A. (2017). The Future of Happiness: 5 Modern Strategies for Balancing Productivity and Well-being in the Digital Era. BenBella Books, Inc..

Blissful. (2020). In Merriam-Webster.com. Retrieved from www.merriam-webster.com/dictio-nary/blissful

Boehm, J. K., Lyubomirsky, S., & Sheldon, K. M. (2011). A longitudinal experimental study comparing the effectiveness of happiness-enhancing strategies in Anglo Americans and Asian Americans. Cognition & Emotion, 25, 1263-1272.

Boehm, J. K., & Lyubomirsky, S. (2008). Does happiness promote career success?. Journal of career assessment, 16(1), 101-116.

Boniwell, I. (2012). Positive Psychology In A Nutshell: The Science Of Happiness: The Science of Happiness. McGraw-Hill Education (UK).

Burns, A. B., Brown, J. S., Sachs-Ericsson, N., Plant, E. A., Curtis, J. T., Fredrickson, B. L., & Joiner, T. E., Jr. (2008). Upward spirals of positive emotion and coping: Replication, extension, and initial explora-tion of neurochemical substrates. Personality and Individual Differences, 44(2), 360-370.

Calling. (2020). In Merriam-Webster.com. Retrieved from www.merriam-webster.com/dictionary/calling

Cameron, K., & Dutton, J. (Eds.). (2003). Positive organizational scholarship: Foundations of a new discipline. Berrett-Koehler Publishers.

Cameron, K. S., & Spreitzer, G. M. (Eds.). (2011). The Oxford handbook of positive organizational scholarship. Oxford University Press.

Coget, Aymee. (2018). Happiness for Humankind Playbook: Sustainable Happiness in 5 Steps.

Cohn, M. A., & Fredrickson, B. L. (2006). Beyond the moment, beyond the self: Shared ground between selective investment theory and the broaden-and-build theory of positive emotions. Psychological Inquiry, 17(1), 39-44.

Czikszentmihalyi, M. (1990). Flow: The psychology of optimal experience. New York: Harper & Row.

Dambrun, M., Després, G., & Lac, G. (2012). Measuring happiness: from fluctuating happiness to authentic–durable happiness. Frontiers in psychology, 3, 16.

David, S. A., Boniwell, I., & Ayers, A. C. (Eds.). (2014). The Oxford handbook of happiness. Oxford University Press.

Deci, E. L., & Ryan, R. M. (1985). Intrinsic motivation and self-determination in human behavior. New York: Plenum.

Cameron, K., & Dutton, J. (Eds.). (2003). Positive organizational scholarship: Foundations of a new discipline. Berrett-Koehler Publishers.

Fowler, J. H., & Christakis, N. A. (2008). Dynamic spread of happiness in a large social network: longitudinal analysis over 20 years in the Framingham Heart Study. Bmj, 337, a2338.

Fredrickson, B. (2009). Positivity: Top-notch research reveals the 3-to-1 ratio that will change your life. Harmony.

Fredrickson, B. L., Cohn, M. A., Coffey, K. A., Pek, J., & Finkel, S. M. (2008). Open hearts build lives: Positive emotions, induced through loving-kindness meditation, build consequential personal resources. Journal of Personality and Social Psychology, 95(5): 1045–1062.

Fredrickson, B. L., & Branigan, C. (2005). Positive emotions broaden the scope of attention and thought-action repertoires. Cognition & emotion, 19(3), 313-332.

Fredrickson, B. L., & Losada, M. F. (2005). Positive affect and the complex dynamics of human flourishing. American psychologist, 60(7), 678.

Fredrickson, B. L. (2004). The broaden–and–build theory of positive emotions. Philosophical Trans-actions of the Royal Society of London. Series B: Biological Sciences, 359(1449), 1367-1377.

Fredrickson, B. L. (2003). The value of positive emotions: The emerging science of positive psychol-ogy is coming to understand why it's good to feel good. American scientist, 91(4), 330-335.

Fredrickson, B. L., & Joiner, T. (2002). Positive emotions trigger upward spirals toward emotional well-being. Psychological science, 13(2), 172-175.

Fredrickson, B. L. (2001). The role of positive emotions in positive psychology: The broad-en-and-build theory of positive emotions. American psychologist, 56(3), 218.

Gandhi, M. (2012). The essential Gandhi: an anthology of his writings on his life, work, and ideas. Vintage.

Hackman, J. R., & Oldham, G. R. (1975). Development of the job diagnostic survey. Journal of Applied psychology, 60(2), 159.

Howell, R. T., Kern, M. L., & Lyubomirsky, S. (2007). Health benefits: Meta-analytically determining the impact of well-being on objective health outcomes. Health Psychology Review, 1(1), 83-136.

Huffman, J. C., Mastromauro, C. A., Boehm, J. K., Seabrook, R., Fricchione, G. L., Denninger, J. W., & Lyubomirsky, S. (2011). Development of a positive psychology intervention for patients with acute cardiovascular disease. Heart international, 6(2), hi-2011.

Layous, K., & Chancellor, J. (2011). Lyubomirsky S, Wang L, Doraiswamy PM. Delivering happiness: translating positive psychology intervention research for treating major and minor depressive disorders. J Altern Complement Med, 17(8), 675-83.

Lyubomirsky, S. (2008). The how of happiness: A scientific approach to getting the life you want. New York: Penguin Press.

Lyubomirsky, S. (2014). The myths of happiness: What should make you happy, but doesn't, what shouldn't make you happy, but does. New York: Penguin Books.

Lyubomirsky, S., King, L., & Diener, E. (2005). The benefits of frequent positive affect: Does happiness lead to success?. Psychological bulletin, 131(6), 803.

Lyubomirsky, S., & Lepper, H. S. (1999). A measure of subjective happiness: Preliminary reliability and construct validation. Social indicators research, 46(2), 137-155.

Lyubomirsky, S. (2001). Why are some people happier than others? The role of cognitive and moti-vational processes in well-being. American psychologist, 56(3), 239.

Lyubomirsky, S., Boehm, J. K., Kasri, F., & Zehm, K. (2011). The cognitive and hedonic costs of dwell-ing on achievement-related negative experiences: Implications for enduring happiness and unhap-piness. Emotion, 11(5), 1152.

Lyubomirsky, S., & Boehm, J. K. (2010). Human motives, happiness, and the puzzle of parenthood: Commentary on Kenrick et al.(2010). Perspectives on Psychological Science, 5(3), 327-334.

Lyubomirsky, S., Dickerhoof, R., Boehm, J. K., & Sheldon, K. M. (2011). Becoming happier takes both a will and a proper way: an experimental longitudinal intervention to boost well-being. Emotion, 11(2), 391.

Oldham, G. R., Hackman, J. R., Smith, K. G., & Hitt, M. A. (2005). How job characteristics theory happened. The Oxford handbook of management theory: The process of theory development.

Orem, S. L., Binkert, J., & Clancy, A. L. (2007). Appreciative coaching: A positive process for change. John Wiley & Sons.

Otake, K., Shimai, S., Tanaka-Matsumi, J., Otsui, K., & Fredrickson, B. L. (2006). Happy people become happier through kindness: A counting kindnesses intervention. Journal of happiness studies, 7(3), 361-375.

Parks, A. C., Della Porta, M. D., Pierce, R. S., Zilca, R., & Lyubomirsky, S. (2012). Pursuing happiness in everyday life: The characteristics and behaviors of online happiness seekers. Emotion, 12(6), 1222.

Peterson, C., & Seligman, M. E. (2004). Character strengths and virtues: A handbook and classification (Vol. 1). Oxford University Press.

Ryan, R. M., Bernstein, J. H., & Brown, K. W. (2010). Weekends, work, and well-being: Psychological need satisfactions and day of the week effects on mood, vitality, and physical symptoms. Journal of social and clinical psychology, 29(1), 95-122.

Ryan, R. M., Huta, V., & Deci, E. L. (2008). Living well: A self-determination theory perspective on eudaimonia. Journal of happiness studies, 9(1), 139-170.

Schwartz, B., Ward, A., Monterosso, J., Lyubomirsky, S., White, K., & Lehman, D. R. (2002). Maximizing versus satisficing: Happiness is a matter of choice. Journal of personality and social psychology, 83(5), 1178.

Seligman, M. E. (2004). Authentic happiness: Using the new positive psychology to realize your potential for lasting fulfillment. Simon and Schuster.

Seligman, M. E. (2012). Flourish: A visionary new understanding of happiness and well-being. Simon and Schuster.

Sheldon, K. M., & Lyubomirsky, S. (2012). The challenge of staying happier: Testing the hedonic adaptation prevention model. Personality and Social Psychology Bulletin, 38(5), 670-680.

Sheldon, K. M., Abad, N., Ferguson, Y., Gunz, A., Houser-Marko, L., Nichols, C. P., & Lyubomirsky, S. (2010). Persistent pursuit of need-satisfying goals leads to increased happiness: A 6-month experi-mental longitudinal study. Motivation and emotion, 34(1), 39-48.

Sheldon, K. M., & Lyubomirsky, S. (2007). Is it possible to become happier?(And if so, how?). Social and Personality Psychology Compass, 1(1), 129-145.

Sheldon, K. M., & Lyubomirsky, S. (2006). How to increase and sustain positive emotion: The effects of expressing gratitude and visualizing best possible selves. The journal of positive psychology, 1(2), 73-82.

Sheldon, K. M., & Lyubomirsky, S. (2006). Achieving sustainable gains in happiness: Change your actions, not your circumstances. Journal of Happiness Studies, 7(1), 55-86.

Shimai, S., Otake, K., Utsuki, N., Ikemi, A., & Lyubomirsky, S. (2004). Development of a Japanese version of the Subjective Happiness Scale (SHS), and examination of its validity and reliability. [Nihon koshu eisei zasshi] Japanese journal of public health, 51(10), 845-853.

Sin, N. L., & Lyubomirsky, S. (2009). Enhancing well-being and alleviating depressive symptoms with positive psychology interventions: A practice-friendly meta-analysis. Journal of clinical psychology, 65(5), 467-487.

Snyder, C. R., & Lopez, S. J. (Eds.). (2009). Oxford handbook of positive psychology. Oxford library of psychology.

Tkach, C., & Lyubomirsky, S. (2006). How do people pursue happiness?: Relating personality, happiness-increasing strategies, and well-being. Journal of happiness studies, 7(2), 183-225.

Tugade, M. M., & Fredrickson, B. L. (2004). Resilient individuals use positive emotions to bounce back from negative emotional experiences. Journal of personality and social psychology, 86(2), 320.

Tugade, M. M., Fredrickson, B. L., & Feldman Barrett, L. (2004). Psychological resilience and positive emotional granularity: Examining the benefits of positive emotions on coping and health. Journal of personality, 72(6), 1161-1190.

Wong, P. T. (2011). What is existential positive psychology?. International Journal of Existential Psychology and Psychotherapy, 3(1).

Wrzesniewski, A. (2003). Finding positive meaning in work. Positive organizational scholarship: Foundations of a new discipline, 296-308.

ABOUT THE AUTHOR: AYMEE COGET, PH.D.

In 1996, Aymee Coget, Ph.D. (pronounced Co-jjayy), made the decision to devote her entire life to helping millions of people live happier lives. Since then, she has established an international practice based in San Francisco teaching happiness science to individuals and groups in addition to giving keynote speeches.

She has over twenty years of experience in positive psychology and teaches people how to be happy and handle life's toughest challenges. She does this through her leadership training program called, The Happi-ness Makeover™. She has received accolades for her work from people who thought they would never experience happiness, as demonstrated in client testi-monials.

Dr. Aymee's combinations of techniques focusing on the mind, body, and spirit have helped people achieve a deep inner contentment that stays regardless of what the situation may bring. Being recognized as a leader in helping others feel better, Dr. Aymee blogs for many websites including Yahoo! Health and Blogher. She consults with global companies on sustainable happiness from perspectives of products, customers, and employees.

She frequently comments on the topics of happiness and resiliency for the media including magazines, newspapers, and television.

In 2004, recognized as a happiness authority by Lionel Ketchian, the founder of The Happiness Club, she was asked to start a happiness club in San Francisco and since then, has trained others on how to lead Happiness Clubs.

Dr. Aymee takes a 'training' approach with her clients by seeing them as whole individuals who need to simply learn to employ the skills of happiness science. With www.happinessforhumankind.com she trains and certifies Happiness Coach-es who undergo intense training in order to facilitate the Happiness Makeover®. Aymee's Ph.D. is in Organizational Psychology with an emphasis in leadership and the science of happiness.

Made in the USA
Monee, IL
18 January 2021